published by

WELLTON BOOKS

P.O. Box 989
Citrus Heights CA 95611

ISBN 0-943678-01-3

Printed in U.S.A

COOKING IN THE NUDE

"Quickies"

Written and illustrated by
Debbie & Stephen Cornwell

"Quickies" is for busy, but romantic, people who love to act out their culinary fantasies. Whenever you need a unique and impressive dinner on short notice, you'll find a "quickie" is the simple and sensual solution.

Creating a gourmet quality dinner in less than an hour would challenge even the great chefs. Often, just searching for the right recipe can take that long, but, we've saved you the effort. Every entre in *Cooking in the Nude, Quickies* can be prepared in an hour or less. How you spend the time you've saved is up to you!

WARNING: While impromptu passion in the dining room can be fun, we must advise you to be 'ready for action' before you start 'fooling around'. Be sure you read both sections before you try anything!

"Quickies" is meant to be spontaneous and fun! Just add enough romance and lust to suit your tastes and enjoy your epicurean conquest!

TABLE OF CONTENTS

READY FOR ACTION! 6-7
(Presentation)

FOOLING AROUND 8
(Creating the Mood)

A LICK AND A PROMISE 9
(Pantry Needs)

TEASING AND PLEASING 10-12
(Appetizers)

LOVE 'EM AND LEAF 'EM 13
(Salads)

FAST AU FARES 14-55
(Entres)

MAKING TIME 56-59
(Vegetables)

INDEX 60-61

FLEETING FANTASIES 62-63
(Notes)

READY FOR ACTION!

(Presentation)

The most pleasureable quickies are often prompted by chance and impulse! As you're leaving work, you run into an old friend (or make a new one) and extend a dinner invitation for that same evening. Or, you are suddenly overcome with the impetus to practice a little culinary seduction on your spouse tonight. Whatever your motives may be, there's very little time for planning or preparation. After all, your desire is to lavish attention on your companion, not in the kitchen!

But, even when timing is tight, the presentation of your epicurean endeavor is still important. Although your entre will be enticing, you still need a sensual table setting, the perfect wine, and the right music to bring out the bon vivant attributes of your guest! To best accomplish this, we suggest you develop a personalized "Quickie Kit". Devote a cupboard in the kitchen or even a section of a closet to those special items of presentation that you're sure to need.

Be ready for action! You don't have time to waste looking for the candle holders! Your "Quickie Kit" should contain; two place settings of provocative dinnerware, napkins (prefolded, in rings), placemats or tablecloth, ice bucket, wine glasses (red and white), candles and holders, silk flowers and vase, a mini-selection (six bottles) of wine, and finally, three or four albums or tapes of appropriately sensuous music. Depending on your style and intentions, you may wish to embelish your "Quickie Kit" with a provocative selection of after dinner pleasures. From backgammon to bubble bath, if you're ready for action, you can indulge with confidence!

FOOLING AROUND

(Creating the Mood)

It's 7:00 and your guest has arrived. Since you're "ready for action", you now have time for a little fooling around! Naturally, your approach to creating the mood will be tailored to fit the relationship, as well as your particular fantasies of the evening. Whether your dining companion is an old friend, a new acquaintance, or your spouse, we're going to presume that your objectives are romantic. How you're dressed may signal your intentions, so be sure that what you're wearing (or not wearing!) truly reflects just how much fooling around you hope to do!

It takes two to fool around, so involve your epicurean partner from the beginning of the evening. Your pre-chosen assortment of wines and music are close at hand. Ask your guest to decant a particular wine, play a special album, and to light the candles. This will allow you time to complete any last minute garnishes and to check on the progress of your gourmet quickie, without seeming rushed. Now's the time to "tease and please" with an appetizer, pour the first glass of wine and, during the conversation that follows, reveal the recipe title of your entree. You've definitely created the mood—where you go from here is up to you!

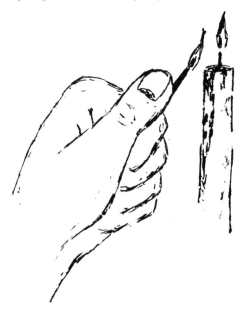

A LICK AND A PROMISE!

A candlelight dinner for two,
will satisfy both of you.
But, when in a hurry
and we've called for curry,
replacing with dill, won't do!

A well stocked pantry is a prerequisite to seductive dining on short notice. The following list of seasonings, condiments, and liquors will allow you to experiment fully with all of our recipes.

anchovy paste	basil
artichoke crowns	bay leaves
artichoke hearts	bouquet garni
black olives	caraway seed
capers	cayenne
chives	celery salt
dried apricots	chervil
fresh ginger	ginger
lemons	marjoram
parsley	paprika
pecans	rosemary
slivered almonds	thyme
walnuts	olive oil
	Dijon mustard

Sherry	Marsala
Port	Kirsh
Brandy	Sauterne (or dry white
Madeira	wine)

Grand Marnier

TEASING AND PLEASING

BITS OF PLEASURE

20 MINUTES

8-12 large cooked, cleaned shrimp
2 T. Roquefort or Bleu cheese
2 T. cream cheese
1 T. mayonaise
1/2 t. thyme
1/2 t. paprika
1/2 t. lemon juice

Blend softened cheese with remaining ingredients. Cut shrimp in half lengthwise leaving tails intact. Stuff shrimp with cheese mixture.

3 T. parsley, minced

Roll rounded backs of shrimp in parsley. Chill until ready to serve.

HOT BAKED BRIE

10 MINUTES

2-4 oz. round Brie cheese
1/4 C. almonds, or finely chopped pecans
1 T. butter

Melt Butter over medium flame. Add nuts and saute' for 5 minutes. Press nuts into soft part of Brie using back of spoon. Bake in covered ceramic or glass dish for 5-7 minutes. Serve immediately with crackers or french bread.

HERBED CHEESE FANTASY

15 MINUTES

1/2 lb Feta cheese
1/2 C. butter, room
temperature
1/4 C. green onion, chopped
1/2 t. anchovy paste
3/4 t. caraway seed
1/4 t. dry mustard

Combine all ingredients, mix thoroughly. Remove mixture to crock, cover, refrigerate. Remove from refrigerator 20 minutes before serving to assure spreadability.

CROWNS OF CRAB

15 MINUTES

STEP ONE:

1.2 C. fresh crab
2-3 T. mayonnaise
1/4 t. worcestershire
1 T. lemon juice
Cayenne pepper, to taste

Mix all ingredients together thoroughly.

STEP TWO:

1 pkg. artichoke crowns
(bottoms), cooked and
drained

Stuff crowns with mound of crab mixture, cover and chill.

FRENCH DIP

30 MINUTES

STEP ONE:

1/2 package Knorr's Leek
  Soup
1 bunch, tops only, green
  onions
1 C. mayonnaise
1 C. sour cream
1 can water chestnuts,
  drained, chopped
1 package frozen chopped
  spinach, cooked and
  squeezed dry
garlic, to taste

Combine all ingredients together
thoroughly.

STEP TWO:

round loaf French bread

Cut a "lid" from top of loaf. Scoop out
bread from inside leaving 1" thickness to
sides and bottom. Fill with dip. Replace
lid, place on serving tray.

STEP THREE:

4-5 large carrots, peeled
  and cut into sticks
1/2 head broccoli, cut into
  flowerettes
1/2 head cauliflower, cut
  into flowerettes
2 zucchini, cut into
  into sticks

Surround bread with vegetable dippers
and serve.

LOVE 'EM AND LEAF 'EM

The evening began with a little 'fooling around' and you moved in quickly with 'teasing' appetizers. A 'fast au fare' is now only moments away, but, let the anticipation build! You can reach the heights of subliminal seduction with your salad! Even in a quickie situation, this brief interlude can be a most satisfying experience if you follow the K.I.S.S. principal to salad making. Keep It Simply Sensual!

You can garnish your greens to reflect your intentions by combining common ingredients in an unusual way. A creative arrangement of olives and carrots could be mildly flirtatious — or boldly suggestive — depending on how you slice them! Compose your salad to best express your desires but, keep it simple and make your own dressing, if possible.

This is a basic honey-lemon dressing whose variety is almost endless.

STEP ONE:

2/3 C. mayonnaise
2 T. vegetable oil
2 T. honey
2 T. half and half
1 T. prepared mustard
1 1/2 T. fresh lemon juice
1/8 t. dry mustard
1 T. parsley, chopped

Combine all ingredients and mix thoroughly.

Try adding any of the following options to the basic dressing and tailor it to your menu.

1/8 t. curry
1 green onion, chopped
1/2 t. celery seeds
1/2 t. poppy seeds
1-2 t. seasame seeds

2 T. raisins
2 T. nuts, slivered almonds,
  chopped pecans, cashews,
or walnuts.
2 t. capers
2 t. chopped black olives

13

TEASING & PLEASING
French Dip

LOVE'EM & LEAF'EM
Lovers Leaves

FAST ALL FARES
Halibut my place?

MAKING TIME
Rosemary Potatoes

Pinot Blanc

HALIBUT MY PLACE?

. . . or your place is fine, wherever you dine you'll have plenty of time!

30 MINUTES

STEP ONE:

2 halibut steaks, 1 " thick
1 T. butter
salt and pepper, to taste

Arrange halibut in au gratin dishes or baking dish. Melt butter and brush over halibut, season to taste. Bake at 450° for 20 minutes.

STEP TWO:

1/4 C. slivered almonds
1 T. butter

Melt butter, add almonds and saute' until golden approximately 10-15 minutes.

STEP THREE:

2 T butter
2 T. flour
1/2 C. milk
1/2 C. sour cream
2 T. fresh lemon juice
2 T. capers, drained
1/4 C. sherry

Melt butter over medium flame, whisk in flour and cook 2 minutes. Whisk in milk, stirring constantly until thickened. Remove from heat. Blend in sour cream, lemon juice, and capers. Pour over fish. Garnish with almonds, parsley, and lemon slices.

LOVERS LURE

Once the lure is set, control your lines, and play with your catch as long as you like!

20 MINUTES

STEP ONE:

2 boned trout, halved
1/2 C. butter
1/4 C. flour
1-2 T. fresh lemon juice
1/2 lemon, sliced

Melt butter over medium high flame in large frypan. Put flour in plastic bag, add trout, one at a time. Shake to coat. Place in pan skin side up, brown 5 minutes. Sprinkle lemon juice over trout. Add lemon slices to pan. Turn trout and brown 1-2 minutes. Remove trout and lemons to heated platter.

STEP TWO:

3/4 C. Grand Marnier
1/3 C. butter, sliced
2 T. parsley, chopped

Pour off any butter in pan, add Grand Marnier. Shake pan, turn flame to low. Ignite Grand Marnier. Allow flames to subside. Whisk butter pieces into pan until sauce thickens. Pour a little sauce over trout, sprinkle with parsley. Pour remaining sauce into serving bowl and pass.

TEASING & PLEASING
Bits of Pleasure

LOVE 'EM & LEAF 'EM
with Asparagus Tips & Mushrooms

FAST AU FARES
LOVERS LURE

MAKING TIME
Bacon Cauliflower Sauté

Chenin Blanc

Crowns of Crab

Suggestive Salad

cop a fillet

Asparagus in Almond Butter

Fumé Blanc

COP A FILLET

. . . and this won't be your only success tonight!

35 MINUTES

STEP ONE:

1/2 C. Sauterne, or dry
   white wine
1/2 onion, thinly sliced
1 bay leaf
1/8 t. thyme
1/2 C. whipping cream

Combine all ingredients in saucepan and boil down to about 2 T. Reduce heat and add cream. Simmer until mixture coats spoon. Approximately 2-3 minutes.

STEP TWO:

1/2 C. butter
1/2 clove garlic, crushed
1/4-1/8 t. minced fresh
   ginger
1 T. parsley, minced
1/2 t. soy sauce
salt and pepper, to taste

Stir butter into cream mixture until blended. Add remaining ingredients. Keep warm.

STEP THREE:

2 T. butter
2 snapper fillets
salt and pepper, to taste

Melt butter in large frypan. Season fillets and fry them on both sides, over medium flame until lightly browned and cooked through.

STEP FOUR:

curly leaf lettuce leaves
lemon wedges
2 T. chopped parsley
3 T. slivered almonds

Arrange lettuce leaves on plate. Top with fillets. Spoon sauce over. Sprinkle with parsley and almonds. Garnish with lemon wedges.

19

GIVE A LITTLE, GET A LITTLE

Be a little shellfish and get all that you can!

35 MINUTES

STEP ONE:

1/4 C. butter
1 clove garlic, minced
1 T. parsley, minced
1 t. Bouquet Garni
2 t. lemon peel, grated
salt and pepper, to taste
1/2 C. dry bread crumbs
1/4 C. Parmesan cheese

Melt butter in large frypan. Saute' garlic for 2 minutes. Remove from flame and add remaining ingredients, toss to coat bread crumbs well. Set aside.

STEP TWO:

2 T. butter
2 T. flour
1 C. half and half or milk
2 T. sherry
salt and pepper, to taste

Melt butter over medium flame. Whisk in flour and cook 2 minutes. Whisk in half and half, stirring constantly until thickened. Whisk in sherry, salt and pepper.

STEP THREE:

1 lb. cooked shrimp

Arrange shrimp in au gratin dishes. Top with sauce, then bread crumbs. Bake at 325° for 20 minutes.

TEASING & PLEASING
Hot Baked Brie

LOVE'EM & LEAF'EM
with Marinated Mushroom Garnish

FAST AU FARES
GIVE A LITTLE, GET A LITTLE

MAKING TIME
Bacon Cauliflower Sauté

Chenin Blanc

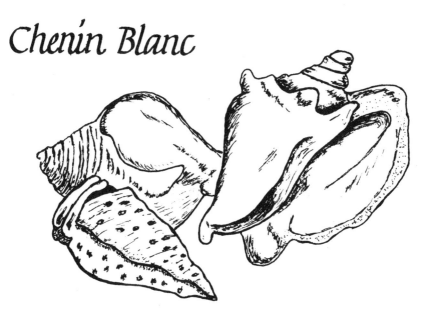

TEASING & PLEASING
Crowns of Crab

LOVE'EM & LEAF'EM
Leaves Garnished with Artichoke Hearts

FAST AU FARES
PROMISCUOUS PRAWNS

MAKING TIME
Parmesan Sprouts

Sauvignon Blanc

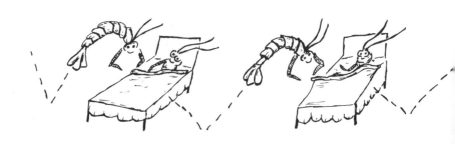

PROMISCUOUS PRAWNS

A dinner of scampi and a good bottle of wine have been known to loosen the inhibitions — just how loose is up to you!

20 MINUTES

STEP ONE:

2-3 T. olive oil
1 clove garlic, minced
2-3 green onions, chopped
8-10 large prawns, cleaned
and butterflied
2/3 C. Sauterne, or dry
white wine
juice of 1/2 lemon
2 T. parsley, chopped
2-3 T. butter

Heat oil in large frypan over medium flame. Saute' garlic and onions until tender. Add prawns and saute' until pink, approx 3 minutes. Add remaining ingredients, butter last. Stir briefly to give sauce a creamy appearance.

STEP TWO:

lemon wedges
parsley sprigs

Remove to warmed au gratin dishes and garnish with lemon and parsley.

CASUAL ENCOUNTERS

are the best kind, and with the right partner, this one could be fantastic!

40 MINUTES

STEP ONE:

1 1/2 C. shell macaroni   Cook and keep warm.

STEP TWO:

1/4 C. butter
3 green onions, chopped
2 T. flour
1 1/2 C. half and half
1/4 C. Madeira
salt and pepper, to taste

Melt butter in large frypan over medium flame, add onion and saute' 3-4 minutes. Whisk in flour and cook 2-3 minutes. Turn flame to low, whisk in half and half, turn flame to medium, continue stirring until sauce thickens. Turn flame to low, whisk in Madeira, salt, and pepper. Keep warm.

STEP THREE:

1 T. lemon juice
2 C. fresh crab meat
1 8 oz. can artichoke hearts, drained
3/4 C. Gruyere, or Swiss cheese, grated

Toss crab with lemon juice. In au gratin dishes, layer well drained macaroni, artichokes, crab, half of the cheese, sauce, and remaining cheese. Bake at 350° for 25 minutes.

Hot Baked Brie

Satiating Salad

CASUAL ENCOUNTERS

Asparagus in
Almond Butter

Pinot Blanc

Bits of Pleasure

Almond & Snow Pea
Garnished Salad

MÉNAGE A TROIS

Julienne of Carrots & Apricots

Gerwertztraminer

MÉNAGE A TROIS

Even when prepared for two, this erotic combo of three seafoods will encourage a lusty appetite!

30 MINUTES

STEP ONE:

4 fillet of sole, pat dry
10 small scallops
3/4 C. crab meat
3/4 C. small cooked shrimp
1/2 C. Monterey Jack
cheese, grated

In buttered au gratin dishes, place one fillet on bottom, top with scallops, crab, shrimp, cheese, and second fillet. Set aside.

STEP TWO:

1/2 C. butter
2 egg yolks
1 T. lemon juice
1/2 t. dry mustard
1/8 t. salt

Melt butter. Place remaining ingredients in bowl. With mixer on high, slowly add butter in steady stream until sauce is thickened and creamy. Pour sauce over fillets and bake at 450° for 10-15 minutes.

STEP THREE:

2 T. parsley, chopped
paprika

Sprinkle parsley over stuffed fillets and dust with paprika.

SKINNY DIPPIN' SHRIMP

*Clothes are optional — or set your own rules — for an evening
of pleasure, this is just one of the tools!*

20 MINUTES

STEP ONE:

2 T. butter 6-8 green onions, chopped 1 clove garlic, minced	Melt butter in large saucepan, over medium flame. Add onions and garlic. Saute' until tender.

STEP TWO:

2 10½ oz. cans cream of potato soup 1 8 oz. package cream cheese 2 cups milk cayenne pepper, to taste	Blend soup and cream cheese into onion mixture until smooth. Add milk and cayenne, blending well.

STEP THREE:

2 C. cleaned, cooked shrimp 1 8 oz. can whole kernel corn, drained	Add shrimp and corn, bring to a boil. Turn flame to medium-low and simmer 10 minutes. Serve.

Hot Baked Brie

Salad with Avocado
& Walnuts

Skinny Dippin Shrimp

Asparagus in Almond Butter

Crisp Chenin Blanc

Bits of Pleasure

Fresh Spinach Salad

CHICKEN PORNO BLEU

Asparagus in Almond Butter

Reisling

CHICKEN PORŃO BLEU

Be careful! This variation of a classic could result in a 'R' rated end to the evening!

45 MINUTES

STEP ONE:

Roquefort cheese
6 oz. cream cheese
3 T. butter
1 clove garlic,
minced
1 T. brandy

Blend garlic and cheeses together, do not overmix. Add butter and brandy and blend well.

STEP TWO:

2 chicken breasts,
skinned and boned

Cover breasts with wax paper and flatten breasts with mallet (¼ " thick). Stuff with cheese mixture. Place on dinner plate, cover with waxed paper and place 2-3 salad plates on top. Refrigerate for 20 minutes.

STEP THREE:

1 egg, beaten
1/3 C. flour
3/4 C. seasoned
bread crumbs

Dip breasts in flour, then in egg, then roll in crumbs. Place in au gratin dishes and bake 20 minutes at 350°.

STEP FOUR:

3 T. butter
1/2 t. each, basil, chervil,
fresh chopped parsley.
1/3 C. Sauterne or other dry
white wine

Melt butter, add herbs and wine. Heat mixture to slow boil. Pour over breasts and serve.

31

LUST AT FIRST BITE

as well as first sight, might make this a lingering sensual night!

30 MINUTES

STEP ONE:

2 boned, skinned chicken
  breasts
salt and pepper to taste

Cover chicken with wax paper and flatten breasts with mallet. Season inside and out with salt and pepper.

STEP TWO:

1 medium ripe banana,
  mashed
1/3 C. orange curacáo or
  Grand Marnier
1 1/2 t. lemon juice
1/4 C. dark corn syrup
1/4 t. salt

Mix all ingredients together and set aside.

STEP THREE:

1/4 C. butter
1/4 C. chopped walnuts
2 T. raisins
1/8 t. salt
1/8 t. pepper
1/2 C. soft bread crumbs

Melt butter. Add remaining ingredients and toss to blend. Stuff chicken breasts with mixture and place in au gratin dishes. Pour half of banana mixture over chicken and bake at 350° for 25-30 minutes, basting once.

STEP FOUR:

1/2 banana, sliced

Top breasts with sliced bananas and spoon sauce over. Return to oven for 2-3 minutes and serve.

Hot Baked Brie

Fruit Fantasies Salad

LUST AT FIRST BITE

Julienne of Carrots
&️ Apricots

Gerwertztraminer

TEASING & PLEASING
Crowns of Crab

LOVE'EM & LEAF'EM
with Snow Peas & Cherry Tomatoes

FAST AU FARES
A quick caper

MAKING TIME
Bacon Cauliflower Sauté

Chenin Blanc

A QUICK CAPER

*like this one, will leave you and your guest plenty of time for any
kind of caper you have in mind!*

20 MINUTES

STEP ONE:

**2 skinned, boned chicken
 breasts**
1/4 C. flour
1/2 t. salt
1/2 t. paprika
1/4 t. pepper

Cover breasts with wax paper and flatten with mallet (¼" thick). Combine flour and spices in plastic bag, add breasts, one at a time, and coat well. Shake off excess.

STEP TWO:

3 T. butter
1 T. olive oil

Heat butter and oil in frypan until bubbling. Add chicken breasts and saute' over medium-high flame, 2-3 minutes per side. Remove to heated platter.

STEP THREE:

2-4 T. Madeira
2-3 T. fresh lemon juice
3 T. capers, drained
3 T. Parsley, chopped
2 T. zest of lemon

Add Madeira to oil/butter and stir up to loosen bits at bottom of pan. Add lemon juice and capers, heat through. Pour over chicken breasts, sprinkle with parsley and lemon zest. Serve immediately.

IT HAD TO BE EWE

*Make it known who **you** had in mind when you serve this entre.*

30 MINUTES

STEP ONE:

3-4 meaty lamb tenderloin chops. 1″ thick, boneless
salt and pepper, to taste
1/2 t. rosemary
2 T. olive oil
2 T. butter

Season chops with salt and pepper, and rosemary. Dust with flour. Melt butter and oil in frypan and brown chops over medium-high flame, until cooked through. Approximately 15 minutes.

STEP TWO:

2 T. flour
1 C. beef stock
1 t. rosemary
salt, to taste
1/2 C. cream
1 T. brandy
2 t. chopped parsley

Remove chops to warmed au gratins or plates. Turn flame to medium and whisk flour into pan juices. Cook for 2 minutes. Whisk in stock. Add rosemary and salt. Return flame to medium-high. Add cream and stir until thickened. Add brandy and pour sauce over chops. Garnish with parsley.

TEASING & PLEASING
Crowns of Crab

LOVE 'EM & LEAF 'EM
Marinated Vegetable Salad

FAST AU FARES
IT HAD TO BE EWE

MAKING TIME
Parmesan Sprouts

Fumé Blanc

TEASING & PLEASING
Hot Baked Brie

LOVE'EM & LEAF'EM
Greens with Fruit & Walnuts

FAST AU FARES
AFFAIRE THEE WELL

Sauvignon
Blanc

AFFAIR THEE WELL

*but, never tell, this quickie could lead to more than
a one-night stand!*

50 MINUTES

STEP ONE:

2 zucchini, sliced julienne 1 small onion, sliced	Cook zucchini and onion in boiling water until crisp-tender. Drain and plunge into ice water. Drain.

STEP TWO:

3-4 1″ lamb tenderloin chops, boneless salt and pepper to taste 3-4 T. Dijon mustard 1/3 C. Port 1/2 C. vegetable broth	Season chops. Brush lightly with mustard. In non-stick frypan, brown chops over high flame, turning once, until done. Remove to heated plate and keep warm. Deglaze pan with Port and reduce liquid to 2 T.. Add broth and simmer until reduced by half.

STEP THREE:

5 T. olive oil 6 artichoke crowns, julienned 2 tomatoes, peeled, coarsly chopped 5 mushrooms, sliced 1/2 C. sliced black olives 3 cloves garlic, minced	Over medium-high flame in large frypan add zucchini, onion, and remaining vegetables. Saute' 5-10 minutes. Arrange on heated plates and top with lamb chops.

STEP FOUR:

2-3 T. butter	Whisk butter into sauce. Add juices left on plate from chops. Pour over lamb and vegetables.

39

TEMPTING TENDER LOINS

The most pleasureable way to overcome a temptation is to yeild to it.

45 MINUTES

STEP ONE:

2-3 boneless pork tenderloin
  chops 1" - 1½" thick
salt and pepper, to taste

Season chops. In non-stick frypan, over high flame, sear chops on both sides. Remove to baking dish.

STEP TWO:

1 C. brown sugar
2/3 C. Kirsh
1/2 C. apple cider

Combine ingredients in sauce pan. cook over medium-high flame, stirring constantly, for 2 minutes. Spoon sauce over chops and bake 25 minutes at 350°.

STEP THREE:

2 T. butter
1/2 C. sliced almonds

Saute' almonds in butter until golden, approximately 10-15 minutes.

STEP FOUR:

2 large apples, sliced thickly
1 T. butter
1/4 C. Sauterne, or other
  dry white wine
1 t. powdered ginger

Melt butter over medium flame. Add apples and saute' briefly. Add wine and ginger, continue cooking until apples are tender.

STEP FIVE:

Remove chops to au gratin dishes. Arrange apples over chops. Pour sauce over and sprinkle with almonds.

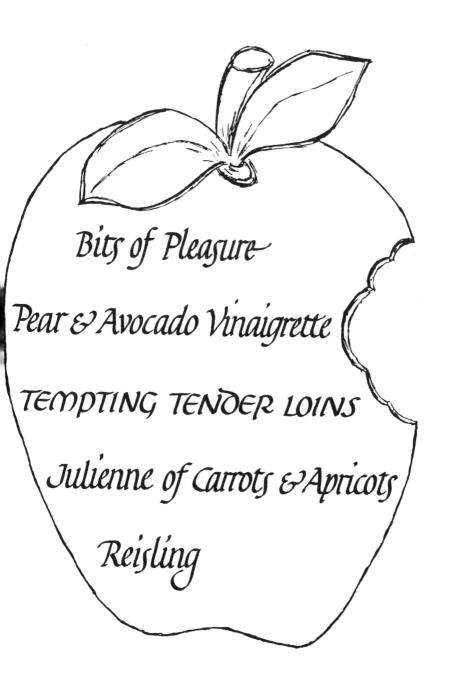

Bits of Pleasure

Pear & Avocado Vinaigrette

TEMPTING TENDER LOINS

Julienne of Carrots & Apricots

Reisling

Herbed Cheese Fantasy

Salad with Artichoke Hearts & Feta Cheese

A SAUCY AFFAIR

Rosemary Potatoes

Sauvignon Blanc

A SAUCEY AFFAIR

may be yours tonight. But, be sure you're ready for more than fooling around!

40 MINUTES

STEP ONE:

2-3 pork tenderloin chops
  1½" thick, boneless
salt and pepper, to taste
1/2 t. marjoram
2 T. olive oil

Season chops on both sides. Heat oil in frypan over high flame and brown chops. Remove to au gratins or baking dish.

STEP TWO:

2 T. butter
1/2 onion, minced
2 T. flour
1 C. Sauterne, or white wine
8-10 mushrooms, sliced
1/2 C. sauerkraut and
  it's juice
1 C. sour cream
1 beef bouillon cube
1/2 t. marjoram

To same pan add butter, heat until sizzling. Add onion and mushrooms and saute' until tender. Turn flame to medium and add flour, cook 2 minutes. Add remaining ingredients, blending well. Pour sauce over chops and bake 30 minutes.

CONSUMING PASSIONS

This selection has never failed to live up to its' name.

45 MINUTES

STEP ONE:

2-4 veal loin chops, boneless
 flattened to 1/4″
1/4 C. flour
salt and pepper, to taste
4 T. butter

Combine flour, salt, and pepper in plastic bag. Add veal scallops one at a time, and coat well, shake off excess. Heat butter over medium-high flame and brown veal on both sides. Approximately 1-2 minutes per side. Remove veal to au gratins or plates and keep warm.

STEP TWO:

2 leeks, chopped
2 shallots, minced
6-8 mushrooms, chopped
3 oz. ham, cut into strips
 (½ c.)
2 T. flour
1 C. milk
salt and pepper, to taste

Saute' leeks and shallots until almost tender, add mushrooms, continue saute'ing until tender. Add ham, whisk in flour, then slowly, add milk, stirring constantly. Bring mixture to a slow boil, lower heat, continue stirring until thickened. Add salt and pepper.

STEP THREE:

3/4 C. Gruyere cheese
 (or Swiss), grated

Sprinkle half the cheese over veal, then half the sauce, then remaining cheese, and sauce, bake 15 minutes at 425°.

Crowns of Crab

Butterleaf Salad Garnished
with Feta

CONSUMING PASSIONS

Julienne of Carrots
& Apricots

Sauvignon Blanc

PASSION IN
PROGRESS

Herbed Cheese Fantasy

Provocative Salad

Bacon Cauliflower
Sauté

Pinot Blanc

VEALING LUSTY?

or vealing loving? Reveal your real vealings tonight!

1 HOUR

STEP ONE:

**2-3 veal scallops, pound
to ⅛″
2-3 thin slices proscuitto
ham
1/4 C. flour
2 T. butter
2 T. olive oil**

Place a slice of ham over each scallop. roll scallops, securing with toothpicks. Dust with flour. Heat oil and butter in frypan, add rolls and saute′ over medium-high flame until browned. Remove veal rolls to heated platter.

STEP TWO:

**2 leeks, chopped
1 shallot, minced
1/2 C. Sauterne, or other
dry white wine
1/4 C. Marsala, or Madeira
2 tomatoes, peeled and
chopped
2 t. basil
salt and pepper, to taste**

Add leeks and shallots to skillet, saute′ over medium flame until tender, 5 minutes. Stir in wine and Marsala, bring to a boil, then turn flame to low. Return veal to pan. Stir in tomatoes, basil, salt and pepper. Cover and simmer 20 minutes. Remove veal to au gratins or plates and spoon sauce over.

VEAL YOU OR VON'T YOU?

Only your true love knows
for sure!

30 MINUTES

STEP ONE:

8-10 mushrooms, thinly
sliced
1/3 C. plus 2 T. dry white
wine
1/2 t. fresh lemon juice
1/8 t. salt
2 T. butter
1 t. flour

Combine 3 T. wine, lemon juice, and salt in small fry pan. Cover and cook over medium-low flame until mushrooms are tender. Blend butter and flour and gradually add to pan, stirring until thickened. Remove from heat.

STEP TWO:

2 T. butter
1 shallot minced
2 leaks, chopped
2-3 boneless veal loin chops-
pounded to 1/4" thickness

Melt butter in large frypan, over medium-high flame. Add shallots and leeks, saute' until tender, about 2-3 minutes. Add veal and quickly brown, about 1-2 minutes. Remove veal, to warmed au gratins or plates. Add remaining wine to pan, scraping up brown bits. Add all to mushroom sauce.

STEP THREE:

1/2 C. whipping cream
lemon juice
salt and pepper, to taste
2-3 T. parsley, chopped

Place sauce over medium-high flame, add cream and bring to a boil until thick and reduced by 1/4. Approximately 2 minutes. Add lemon, salt, and pepper to taste. Pour sauce over veal, sprinkle with parsley.

48

French Dip

Pleasure Seeking Salad

VEAL YOU OR VON'T YOU?

Parmesan Sprouts

Gamay
Beaujolais

French Dip

Fresh Garden Salad

FONDUE ME, PLEASE!

Rosemary Potatoes

Cabernet Sauvignon

FONDUE ME, PLEASE!

with a gentle caress, this dish could lead from a 'maybe' to 'yes'.

30 MINUTES

STEP ONE:

1 lb. lean tenderloin of beef trimmed of fat, cut in bite-size cubes	Mound beef cubes on dinner plates, cover and refrigerate.

STEP TWO:

Madeira-mushroom Sauce

2 T. butter **2 green onions, thinly sliced** **1 leek, thinly sliced** **3 C. finely diced mushrooms** **1/2 C. Madeira** **1 10½ oz. can beef broth**	Melt butter in large saucepan, add onion, leek, and mushrooms and saute' until tender. Add Madeira and broth and simmer over medium-high flame until reduced by half. Approximately 5 minutes.

STEP THREE:

2 T. butter **2 T. flour** **salt and pepper, to taste**	Melt butter in small fry pan over medium-low flame. Whisk in flour and cook 2 minutes. Add to mushroom mixture, stirring until sauce thickens. Season to taste. Serve in individual small bowls.

STEP FOUR:

peanut oil **1/4 C. butter**	Fill fondue pot to 1/3 full with peanut oil. Add butter. On stove, heat until sizzling. Transfer pot to fondue stand, light flame, keep hot.

?   ?   ?

We named the rest of the menus, now it's your turn . . . . Be
Daring!

40 MINUTES

STEP ONE:

1 lb. coarse chopped sirloin 1 egg 1 shallot, minced 1 leek, chopped pepper, to taste	Combine all ingredients, mix thoroughly, shape into six balls. Set aside.

STEP TWO:

6 oz. Roquefort or Bleu cheese 6 oz. cream cheese 1 T. butter 1 T. brandy 1 clove garlic, minced	Combine all ingredients, mix thoroughly. Divide into 6 balls and stuff into beef balls, making sure to totally enclose cheese. Flatten balls slightly.

STEP THREE:

1/2 lb. spinach noodles 2-3 T. butter	Cook noodles, drain, toss with butter. Arrange noodles in au gratin dishes and keep warm.

STEP FOUR:

3 T. butter	Melt butter over medium flame in frypan. Saute' beef until done, Arrange beef over noodles. Keep warm.

STEP FIVE:

6 mushrooms, sliced 1/2 C. Port 3-4 T. capers, drained 1/2 C. whipping cream 1/4 C. butter salt and pepper, to taste	Saute' mushrooms in remianing butter over medium-flame until tender. Whisk in Port, cream, and capers until sauce thickens. Add butter a little at a time. Season and spoon sauce over beef and noodles.

52

French Dip

Sensuous Salad

? ? ?

Rosemary Potatoes

Brussel Sprouts in
  Garlic-Parmesan Butter

Gamay Beaujolais

TEASING & PLEASING
Herbed Cheese Fantasy

LOVE'EM & LEAF'EM
with Shrimp Garnish

FAST AU FARES
FETTISHCHINI

Pinot Noir

FETTISH—CHINI

Who knows what fettishes lurk in your true loves' heart? Do you?

40 MINUTES

STEP ONE:

8 slices bacon, chopped

Fry bacon until crisp. Remove with slotted spoon and drain on paper towels.

STEP TWO:

1/2 lb. fettuchini
1/4 C. butter

Cook fettuchini until al dente. Drain and toss with butter in large serving bowl. Set aside, keep warm.

STEP THREE:

3-5 mushrooms, sliced
1 large carrot, sliced
1/2 C. cauliflower, sliced
1/2 C. frozen peas
1 medium zucchini, sliced
4 green onions, sliced
1 clove garlic, minced

Add vegetables to bacon drippings in frypan and saute' over medium-high flame until crisp-tender.

STEP FOUR:

4 eggs
1/4 C. whipping cream
1 C. fresh Parmesan, grated
salt and pepper, to taste

Beat eggs and cream together until blended. Toss with fettuchini. Add vegetables, bacon, Parmesan, salt and pepper, toss again.

BACON CAULIFLOWER SAUTE'

15 MINUTES

STEP ONE:

4-5 slices bacon, chopped

In large frypan, over medium-high flame, fry bacon until crisp. Remove with slotted spoon and drain on paper towels.

STEP TWO:

1/2 head cauliflower, cut into flowerettes.
1/2 t. celery salt
1 T. chopped chives

Saute' cauliflower in bacon drippings over medium flame until lightly browned on all sides. Add celery salt and toss. Remove to serving bowl. Toss with bacon and chives.

BRUSSEL SPROUTS
IN GARLIC-PARMESAN BUTTER

15 MINUTES

STEP ONE:

1/2 lb brussel sprouts, cleaned and trimmed

Steam sprouts until tender, about 15 minutes. Keep warm.

STEP TWO:

2 T. butter
1 clove garlic, minced
1/4 C. fresh parmesan cheese, grated
salt and pepper, to taste

Melt butter in frypan over medium-flame. Saute' garlic 2 minutes. Drain sprouts, add to butter, toss to coat evenly. Add parmesan, toss again. Season to taste, toss again. Remove to serving bowl.

GARLIC ROSEMARY POTATOES

30 MINUTES

STEP ONE:

**2 large baking potatoes,
peeled, sliced ½" thick
1/4 C. butter
2-3 T. rosemary, crushed
garlic salt, to taste
pepper, to taste**

Spread potatoes on greased baking sheet. Melt butter and brush half of butter on potatoes. Sprinkle with rosemary, garlic salt and pepper. Bake at 375° until golden, approximately 10 minutes. Turn, brush with remaining butter, season with rosemary, garlic, and pepper and bake until golden and crisp.

ASPARAGUS IN ALMOND-LEMON BUTTER

25 MINUTES

STEP ONE:

**1/2 lb pencil size asparagus
spears**

Steam asparagus until crisp-tender.

STEP TWO:

**1/4 C. butter
1/4 C. sliced almonds
1 T. lemon juice**

Melt butter in saucepan over medium flame. Saute' almonds until golden. Add lemon juice and blend well. Serve over asparagus spears.

JULIENNE OF CARROTS AND APRICOTS

20 MINUTES

STEP ONE:

2 T. butter
1 shallot, cut into strips
1/2 lb carrots, grated
6 dried apricots, cut into
 strips
1/2 C. vegetable or chicken
 broth
1 T. wine vinegar

Melt butter in frypan over medium-high flame. Add shallot and saute' until tender. Add carrots and apricots and saute' 2-3 minutes. Add stock, cover, and simmer until carrots are crisp tender. Uncover and simmer until all liqued evaporates. Sprinkle with vinegar.

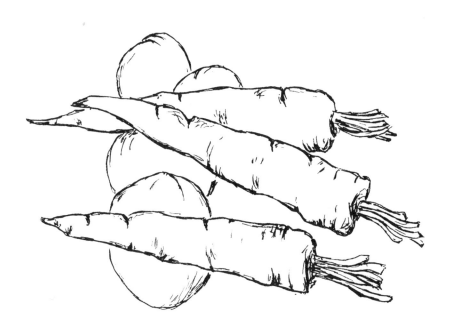

INDEX

TEASING AND PLEASING: *(Appetizers)*

Bits of Pleasure 10
    Stuffed Shrimp
Hot Baked Brie 10
    Brie Cheese Rolled in Nuts and Baked
Herbed Cheese Fantasy 11
    Herbed Cheese Spread
Crowns of Crab 11
    Crab Stuffed Artichoke Crowns
French Dip 12
    Leek Dip in a French Bread Bowl

LOVE 'EM AND LEAF 'EM: *(Salads)* 13

FAST AU FARES: *(Entres)* 14-55

BEEF AND VEAL:

Fondue Me, Please! 51
    (Beef Fondue with Mushroom Madeira Sauce)
? ? ? 52
    (Roquefort Stuffed Beef in Caper Sauce)
Vealing Lusty? 47
    (Veal and Ham Rolls in Tomato Basil Sauce)
Consuming Passions. 44
    (Veal in Rich Cream Sauce)
Veal You or Von't You? 48
    (Veal in Mushroom Cream Sauce)

CHICKEN:

Chicken Porino Blue 31
    (Roquefort Stuffed Breasts in Wine and Herb Sauce)
A Quick Caper 35
    (Chicken Breasts in Caper Madeira Sauce)
Lust At First Bite 32
    (Stuffed Breasts with Banana Grand Marnier Sauce)

FISH AND SEAFOOD:

Halibut My Place? 15
  (Halibut in Cream Caper Sauce)
Lovers Lure 16
  (Trout Fillets in Grand Marnier Sauce)
Cop A Fillet 19
  (Snapper Fillets in Ginger Cream Sauce)
Give A Little, Get A Little 20
  (Shrimp in Wine Sauce with Herb Topping)
Promiscuous Prawns 23
  (Scampi in Garlic Wine Sauce)
Casual Encounters 24
  (Crab and Artichokes in Madeira Cream Sauce)
Ménage A Tróis 27
  (Sole Stuffed with Scallops, Crab, and Shrimp)
Skinny Dippin' Shrimp 28
  (Rich Shrimp Chowder)

LAMB:

It Had To Be Ewe 36
  Lamb Chops in Rosemary Brandy Sauce)
Affaire Thee Well 39
  Lamb Chops in Wine Sauce with sauteéd vegetables)

PORK:

Tempting Tender Loins 40
  (Tenderloins of Pork and Apples in Kirsh Glaze)
A Saucy Affair 43
  (Pork Tenderloins in Sour Cream Sauce)

PASTA:

Fettish-chini 55
  (Fettuchini and Sauteed Vegetables)

VEGETABLES:

Bacon Cauliflower Saute' 56
Brussel Sprouts in Garlic Parmesan Butter 57
Garlic Rosemary Potatoes 58
Asparagus in Almond Lemon Butter 58
Julienne of Carrots and Apricots 59

FLEETING FANTASIES

FLEETING FANTASIES